Miles Standish

Plymouth Colony Leader

Colonial Leaders

Lord Baltimore *English Politician and Colonist*

Benjamin Banneker *American Mathematician and Astronomer*

William Bradford *Governor of Plymouth Colony*

Benjamin Franklin *American Statesman, Scientist, and Writer*

Anne Hutchinson *Religious Leader*

Cotton Mather *Author, Clergyman, and Scholar*

William Penn *Founder of Democracy*

John Smith *English Explorer and Colonist*

Miles Standish *Plymouth Colony Leader*

Peter Stuyvesant *Dutch Military Leader*

Revolutionary War Leaders

Benedict Arnold *Traitor to the Cause*

Nathan Hale *Revolutionary Hero*

Alexander Hamilton *First U.S. Secretary of the Treasury*

Patrick Henry *American Statesman and Speaker*

Thomas Jefferson *Author of the Declaration of Independence*

John Paul Jones *Father of the U.S. Navy*

Thomas Paine *Political Writer*

Paul Revere *American Patriot*

Betsy Ross *American Patriot*

George Washington *First U.S. President*

Colonial Leaders

Miles Standish

Plymouth Colony Leader

Susan Martins Miller

Arthur M. Schlesinger, jr.
Senior Consulting Editor

Chelsea House Publishers

Philadelphia

Produced by Robert Gerson Publisher's Services

CHELSEA HOUSE PUBLISHERS
Editor in Chief Stephen Reginald
Production Manager Pamela Loos
Director of Photography Judy L. Hasday
Art Director Sara Davis
Managing Editor James D. Gallagher

Staff for *MILES STANDISH*
Project Editor Anne Hill
Project Editor/Publishing Coordinator Jim McAvoy
Contributing Editor Amy Handy
Associate Art Director Takeshi Takahashi
Series Design Keith Trego

The Chelsea House World Wide Web address is http://www.chelseahouse.com

First Printing
1 3 5 7 9 8 6 4 2

Library of Congress Cataloging-in-Publication Data

Miller, Susan Martins.
Miles Standish / by Susan Martins Miller.
    p.   cm. — (Colonial leaders)
Includes bibliographical references and index.
Summary: Presents a biography of the courageous leader who arrived in
America on the Mayflower and led the defense of Plymouth Colony.
ISBN 0–7910–5350-4 (HC)   0–7910–5693-7 (PB)
1. Standish, Miles, 1584?–1656 Juvenile literature.   2. Massachusetts—History—
New Plymouth, 1620–1691 Biography Juvenile literature.   3. Soldiers—
Massachusetts Biography Juvenile literature.   4. Pilgrims (New Plymouth
Colony) Juvenile literature.   [1. Standish, Miles, 1584?–1656.   2. Soldiers.
3. Pilgrims (New Plymouth Colony)   4. Massachusetts—History—New Plymouth,
1620-1691.] I. Title. II. Series.
F68.S865 1999
974.4'01'092—dc21
[B]   99–20977
                                                   CIP

Publisher's Note: In Colonial and Revolutionary War America, there were no standard rules for spelling, punctuation, capitalization, or grammar. Some of the quotations that appear in the Colonial Leaders and Revolutionary War Leaders series come from original documents and letters written during this time in history. Original quotations reflect writing inconsistencies of the period.

Contents

One of the most famous ships of all time,
the Mayflower set sail from England in 1620
with more than 100 passengers. These people
hoped to make new lives for themselves in
the New World. This modern-day replica
shows what the ship looked like.

Captain Shrimp

aptain Shrimp was not always a captain. Once he was a little boy with red hair and a fiery temper. He was not afraid of anything. He was not afraid to fight. He even liked to fight. He was independent and quick-thinking. When he faced a challenge, he was ready for it.

Captain Shrimp was the nickname that people later gave to Miles Standish. He was born about 1584 in Chorley, Lancashire, England. When he was only a boy, his parents died. He was left to take care of himself, and that is exactly what he did. While he was learning to take care of himself, he also learned to be brave, bold, and prepared for anything. He was ready to explore the world.

Even his named suited him. "Miles" is a Latin word that means "soldier." And a soldier is what Miles Standish became. By the time he was 20 years old, he made his living by being a soldier.

Queen Elizabeth I was ruling England. She sent some English troops to Holland to help the Dutch soldiers fight their war against Spain. Miles Standish was one of the soldiers who went to Holland to fight. His own country was not involved in the war. It did not matter to him which side won the war. He was a professional soldier, and his job was to fight for the side which Queen Elizabeth chose.

While Miles Standish was in Holland, he met some other people who had come from England. He did not have very much in common with these people. Miles Standish was not religious, and these people were very strict in their religion. Miles was a professional soldier, and the people he met wanted to live peacefully and simply. Miles had come to Holland to fight in a war; the other people had come to get away from their fights with the **Church of England.**

The people Miles met were called **Puritans**. They had separated from the Church of England, then some of the Puritans separated again. They were not happy even with the Puritans. This group became known as **Separatists** and moved to Holland. They wanted to practice their religion their own way. Their leader was their pastor, John Robinson.

A few years later, the Separatists decided that they had to move again. This time they were going to move far away from England, and far away from Holland. They decided they would go to the New World—to America. In America they would be able build a town and worship freely. No one from the Church of England would tell them what they should believe or what they should do.

But these people knew that they needed more people than just their group of Separatists. There were some farmers and skilled people in the group, but if they were going to build a town, they needed people with many different talents. So they looked for other people to make the journey with them. They found some people who could not find jobs in England. They also found people who just wanted an exciting adventure.

The Separatists had heard reports from people who had already visited the New World so they knew that their new homeland could be dangerous. The Native Americans might be unfriendly or even violent. The other Europeans who were already in the New World might offer little assistance. The **Pilgrims** knew they needed to have someone in their group who could protect them. When the time came to make the journey across the ocean, John Robinson remembered Miles Standish. A professional soldier was just what the group needed.

Miles was married, but he had no other family. He and his wife, Rose, agreed to join the Separatists as they crossed the ocean. Miles had been a soldier in England and Europe. Perhaps he was curious about what the New World was like. Perhaps he wanted a new adventure. Perhaps he was ready to stop being just a soldier and start being a leader. He was about 36 years old when he decided to join the Separatists.

The Separatists did not have enough money to go to the New World. They needed some partners who could help pay for a ship to carry them on the seas. The journey would be a long one. They needed supplies to last several months. They would have to take food and tools and guns. John Robinson arranged for some merchants to invest in the trip. In return, the Separatists would work for seven years to send back furs and other goods that the merchants could sell in England.

The Separatists now became "Pilgrims," because they were taking a journey to a new land. They called themselves the **"Saints"** because they had a religious reason for the journey. The other people who came with them were referred to as the **"Strangers."** The

Pilgrims sincerely hoped that the Strangers would join their religious group.

Miles Standish earned the nickname "Captain Shrimp" because he was short and stocky, with red hair and a red beard. When he lost his temper, which he did often, his face turned red, too. His enemies said, "A little chimney is soon fired," because Miles lost his temper very quickly and became very angry. But the men who worked with Miles knew that he was dependable. They could trust him and could count on him to do his job well. Even though he was not a Pilgrim, he soon became one of the leaders of the group of people planning the long journey.

On September 6, 1620, the *Mayflower* left England with 102 passengers aboard. About 30 sailors helped to operate the boat. The group had hoped to take two ships, but the *Speedwell* was leaky and could not make the trip. The journey was hard. The *Mayflower* had too many people on it, and the sleeping area was very crowded. When people got seasick they had no

Seeking the religious freedom they could not find in England or in Holland, the Pilgrims journeyed to America. A deeply religious people, they prayed for safe passage before the voyage.

place to go. There was no place to take a bath or wash clothes. They had to be careful about how much food and water they used each day.

After more than two months at sea, the first glimpse of land must have been a welcome sight to everyone aboard the *Mayflower* as they neared the coast of Massachusetts.

There was no heat. The people ate salted beef or pork, dried peas, salt fish, and hard biscuits.

The trip began smoothly, but the weather

turned bad. The wind tossed the _Mayflower_ on the ocean waves as if it were a paper boat. The passengers were soaked and cold. Some of them wanted to turn around and go home. But the captain of the ship said they were already more than halfway to the New World. It was too late to turn back.

Finally, after 66 days at sea, the Pilgrims spotted land. But the _Mayflower_ did not land where it was supposed to land. They were far away from their goal. Now they had to decide whether to keep going or stay where they were. Because it was November and winter was beginning, the Pilgrims decided they would stay where they were. Miles Standish helped to make the decision to settle in Provincetown.

The Saints and the Strangers disembarked at Provincetown, Massachusetts, unsure exactly what they would find in the new land and how safe they would be.

Discoveries in a New Land

Both the Saints and the Strangers were relieved to find land. They were glad to choose a place to settle down, but they knew their work was just beginning. In England and Holland, they had had homes. They could go to shops to buy the things they needed. There were towns and cities with enough people to do everything that needed to be done. But in the New World they had very little.

A few Europeans had been to the New World before the *Mayflower* arrived there. They were fur traders and others who would send goods back to England and other countries in Europe. A man named John Smith had made a map of the area where the Pilgrims landed. But it was still a wilderness.

No one had tried to build a town in the wilderness. This is what the Pilgrims wanted to do. They also knew they needed some laws in a land that had none. Some of the leaders wrote the **Mayflower Compact** as soon as they found land. On November 11 most of the men in the group signed it. (At the time of the *Mayflower,* women usually were not allowed to sign important documents.)

The Mayflower Compact explained how the group would work and live together. They wanted to build a **colony** where everyone could live and care for one another. Even though he was not a Saint, Miles Standish was one of the first people to sign the agreement.

It was Miles Standish's job to help explore the wilderness. The Pilgrims needed to find fresh water that they could drink. The food on their ship was running out. They could not keep living on the crowded *Mayflower.* They needed to build houses.

To establish laws to live by in their new home, the Pilgrim leaders composed the Mayflower Compact, which most of the men signed.

The most important part of Miles Standish's job was to find out if any Native Americans lived near the Pilgrims. The Pilgrims hoped the Indians would be friendly, but they were not sure. They depended on Miles to keep them safe.

Miles Standish led the Pilgrims on three "discoveries." A discovery was a trip that the Pilgrim men made to explore their new home. Miles took about 15 men with him on each discovery, including some of the Pilgrim leaders. They needed to make decisions about where to build the new colony. Miles Standish began the *Mayflower* journey as a soldier who worked for the Pilgrims, yet by the time they arrived in the New World he had become one of the group's leaders. Even though he was not a Pilgrim, the leaders trusted his judgment.

The first discovery that Miles went on hap-

Many people think the Pilgrims' first homes were log cabins, but log cabins were not built until much later. The Pilgrims built their houses out of **wattle and daub**, a framework of woven rods and twigs covered and plastered with clay. Their first homes were simple cottages with one large room and thatched roofs. Later many added a **lean-to** on one side for storage.

When it came time to build, the colonists constructed cottages with thatched roofs, like the ones they had known in England.

pened only two days after the *Mayflower* arrived in the New World. The men were disappointed that they did not find fresh water, since after more than two months at sea the colonists desperately needed a drinking source.

Miles and the others did cut firewood and take it back to the ship. Now the settlers would be able to warm themselves in the harsh November weather. They also found a basket of corn. This meant that the Native Americans were nearby. The Pilgrims needed food badly. They decided to take the basket of corn. Later, when they found the Native Americans, they would find a way to pay for the corn.

In order to explore more, the Pilgrims needed to repair their **shallop**. This was a small boat that could be rowed or sailed along the shoreline. While it was being repaired, Miles and the others continued exploring on foot.

On the second discovery, Miles found some homes made of saplings. They had fireplaces and mats and baskets of acorns, fish, and herring. But there were no people. Once again, the Pilgrims looked for fresh water. They dressed in heavy armor and carried **muskets** and swords. They wanted to be ready for anything that might happen. They saw a few Native Americans, who ran when they saw the Pilgrims. The Pilgrims tried to chase them. They wanted to meet them but they could not catch them. Finally, the Pilgrims found a spring of fresh water.

The Pilgrims helped themselves to a basket of the Indians' corn, intending to pay them back later on.

After the shallop was repaired, Miles and the others set out on the third discovery. One day they saw some Native Americans on a nearby beach. The Pilgrims were disappointed that they had not seen them sooner. But they also did not trust them. At night they built a barricade of logs around their camp. About midnight a loud, frightened cry woke them up. The sentry shouted that he had seen Native Americans, but now they were gone. Everyone tried to go back to sleep. At 5:00 in the morning, they got up again. While breakfast was cooking, some of the men started to carry their things down to the shallop on the beach. Some of them left their muskets in the boat when they came back for breakfast. Miles Standish did not approve of this. What if they were caught unprepared?

Suddenly they heard the strange cries of the Indians. One of the Pilgrims on the beach ran toward the group. Arrows flew around his head. Miles flew into action. He had a **flintlock** with him. This meant he could fire his musket almost immediately. Some of the other men were not prepared. They ran to the shallop to get their muskets and fumbled to fire them. Native Americans jumped out of the woods and began to shoot arrows. But the Indians were soon frightened by the musket fire. Most of them ran away.

One of the Native Americans stayed behind and kept shooting arrows. He hid behind a tree, but Miles found him. Miles did not want to kill the Indian, but he certainly wanted him to stop shooting arrows! Miles shot his musket at the tree. Bark splintered up and flew around the man's face. He shrieked and finally ran away.

On December 16, 1620, the Pilgrims discovered a quiet, protected harbor. Six years earlier, John Smith had named this place Plymouth. The harbor had all the fresh water they needed. It was full of fish and water fowl that they could eat. They could have mussels and crabs and lobsters.

They decided that this was the place where they would build their town. Soon they began to measure the area to build a street and houses. Six weeks had passed since they had first sighted land. The discoveries were over. Now it was time to build.

At Plimouth Plantation, a modern re-creation of Plymouth Colony, visitors can see what life was like for the Pilgrims by exploring the buildings and observing performers pretending to be colonists.

Working Together

3

The Plymouth Colony began to look like a town. The work was slow, but everyone was willing to work hard. The new townspeople decided to build 19 cottages and a common house (a building that everyone could use), so that each family would have a small house and there would be a building shared by all. The men who were not married would live with the families. Later they could build their own homes.

Many of the people still lived on the *Mayflower*. They carried supplies from the boat to the land when they needed them. Because the water in the harbor was shallow, the boat could not come very close to land. The Pilgrims had to walk a mile and a half through the water to get from the boat to the land. It was winter time. The water was icy, and the air was windy and cold.

People started to get sick. At first it was just a few, but soon many of the settlers were ill. They did not have nourishing food. They did not have proper buildings for warmth. Walking back and forth through the icy water was not easy. A common house was the first building they needed. The Pilgrims built as quickly as they could. The men started to build the common house on Christmas day in 1620. They cut down trees and split them into boards. Working in the snow and sleet and wind, they raised the frame. They built clay walls and a thatched roof. All the workers knew they were racing against winter, and if they did not win, they would die.

The common house gave them a place to have meetings. They also used it to store some supplies, including gunpowder and muskets. And it was a place where the sick could be taken care of. The common house soon became a hospital.

On January 14, 1621, the common house was full of sick people. There was no room for anyone else in the building. Suddenly, a spark flew up from the fireplace and caught the thatched roof, which was made of grass and other plants. It caught fire very easily. The wind was blowing very hard that day. In only minutes the fire spread through the common house.

Many of the sick people were too weak to get up and go outside. The well people had to help them. But many of the people who were not sick were still on the *Mayflower*. When they saw the smoke of the fire, they rowed the shallop toward land as quickly as they could.

Miles Standish was one of the few people on shore who was not sick. He saw the danger that everyone was in. If the fire reached the barrels of gunpowder, an explosion would kill everyone. He acted as quickly as he could. He worked with some other leaders to get the sick people

The Pilgrims realized they needed a way to protect the colony and they chose Miles Standish (shown here second from left) to lead their small army.

out of the common house and put the fire out as fast as they could.

No one was killed in the fire. But the building was damaged, and the sick became sicker. Many items stored in the common house were destroyed, and there was no way to replace them.

The Pilgrims knew they had no time to waste. If they were going to survive the winter, they all had to work together. A few days after the fire the leaders met to organize a small army. They only had a few dozen men, but they agreed that Miles Standish should command the army. Everyone had to help protect the colony.

A strange interruption stopped the meeting. While the men were talking, two Native Americans appeared on the top of a nearby hill, across a brook. Their faces were brightly painted. With their hands they made signs that the Pilgrims should come up to meet them. The Pilgrim leaders were not sure that was a good idea. They made signs that the Native Americans should come down the hill. The Pilgrims did not move. The Native Americans did not move.

Miles Standish had been eager for some friendly contact with the Indians. He wanted to be careful and wise. His job was to protect the settlers, not to put them in danger. He decided to go to the Native Americans.

Miles and one other man walked toward the hill. They waded through the brook. They laid their muskets on the ground as a sign of peace. When they got close, Miles could hear many more Native Americans out of sight on the hill. He hoped he would get to meet their leaders. But the two Indians who had stood on the hill turned and ran when Miles got close to them.

Native Americans had known other Europeans who had come to their land. They often traded furs and beads with the Europeans. Some Europeans were kind to them, and some were cruel. Some treated them fairly, but others stole from them. At first the Indians must have wondered whether the Pilgrims would be their friends or their enemies.

Miles knew that the Pilgrims must be prepared for when the Native Americans might come back. Next time more than two might come, and they might not be peaceful. He decided to build his fort and get his cannons off the ship as quickly as possible.

The new colony had one street, which ran to

the foot of a steep hill. Everyone agreed that Miles Standish should build a fort on the hill and mount his cannons. They also decided he should build his house at the bottom of the hill. If danger came, he could quickly get to the fort. The settlers called the hill Fort Hill. The men dragged a cannon from the ship and mounted it on a wooden platform on Fort Hill. They also had two other cannons that were smaller. Miles did not know where the Native Americans might come from. He pointed cannons both at the water and at the land.

After the fire, disease spread through the colony like wildfire. In the icy, snowy winter, it was easy to catch pneumonia. Some of the Pilgrims got tuberculosis. Soon people began dying. Two or three people died each day.

On January 29, 1621, Miles Standish's wife, Rose, died. Miles was one of the people who never got sick. But he spent a lot of time taking care of people who did get sick. He had to fetch wood for fires to keep them warm, cook food,

As seen in the modern re-creation, Plymouth Colony had only one street, with all the buildings along its edge.

feed, and wash them. And when they died, it was his job to bury them. When his own wife died, he could not stop and grieve. There was too much to do for everyone else.

Miles was always watchful to see if Native Americans were nearby. But he had to concentrate on keeping the settlers alive. By the end of the winter, half the people who sailed on the *Mayflower* were dead. Barely 50 people were still alive.

As the Pilgrims and Native Americans got to know each other, they often traded goods and helped one another.

4

Friendly
Neighbors

When the colony got smaller in number, the people who were left worked harder. They held another meeting. They had already chosen Miles Standish as their military leader, but they had many more decisions to make.

Once again, their meeting was interrupted. During the first meeting the two Native Americans had stood on a hill to watch the Pilgrims. They did not want to get close. At the second meeting, one Indian walked right into the meeting. He did not seem to be afraid at all. He was a tall man, with long jet-black hair hanging down the back. He walked boldly down the one street of Plymouth colony until he came face to face with the leaders. All the colonists wondered how they would communicate with a Native American. Imagine their surprise when he spoke to them.

"Welcome, Englishmen," he said in plain English. "I am Samoset."

Miles Standish was alert and ready to defend the Pilgrims. But there was no need to be afraid. Samoset was very friendly. He asked for something to drink. The Pilgrims gave him water, biscuits, butter, cheese, pudding, and a piece of mallard (a kind of duck).

Samoset had traded goods with English sea captains. He had even sailed with them on their ships. Along the way, he learned to speak English. He told the Pilgrims that the Native American tribe who had lived in the area around Plymouth had all died from a plague.

Samoset stayed all night in the Plymouth colony. The Pilgrim leaders had many questions about their new home. Samoset answered their questions.

An Indian named Samoset knew how to speak English, and came to give a friendly greeting to the Pilgrims.

The next morning, Samoset left. He told the Pilgrims he would bring back some Native Americans from the Wampanoag tribe. He brought back five warriors. They ate the food the Pilgrims offered. To show their appreciation, they danced for the settlers. They did not know that the Pilgrims did not approve of dancing!

Captain Standish saw that the five Indians had some tools that belonged to the Pilgrims. The tools had disappeared a few weeks earlier. Miles knew that some Native Americans must have taken them, but he did not know how to get them back. Without their tools, the Pilgrims would not be able to build their town. Miles was relieved when the Native Americans finally offered to give the tools back. Then he urged the Native Americans to bring them all the beaver furs they could. The settlers could send the furs to England to help pay their debt to the **adventurers**.

Once the Indians were gone, Captain Standish called another meeting. They still needed to fin-

When the Europeans came to North America, they brought many weapons, such as muskets and cannons. But the worst threat they brought was their disease. The Native Americans had no resistance to diseases from Europe, so they were easily infected. The tribe that had lived near Plymouth probably died from smallpox.

ish making decisions about how to organize their army. So far, all the Native Americans they had met were friendly. But they could not be sure the next ones would be kind.

Once again two Native Americans appeared on the hill. They seemed to dare the Pilgrims to come after them. Captain Standish was tired of playing games. He took his musket and splashed angrily across the brook toward the Native Americans. The two men made faces at him, but they left.

Miles and the Pilgrims went back to their meeting. For a third time, they were interrupted. Samoset was back. This time he brought another man, Squanto. He said that Squanto had been in England. He could speak better English than Samoset.

They brought word that Chief Massasoit was near. He was bringing 60 warriors with him. The Pilgrims knew the Native Americans were not out hunting. But what did they want? Captain Standish quickly formed his men into ranks. He made sure that their most powerful weapons were ready.

At first the Pilgrims and the Native Americans were not sure they could trust each other. Squanto carried messages back and forth. The Pilgrims sent a message that they wanted to be peaceful and trade with the Wampanoags. They sent a gift of knives and a copper chain to Chief Massasoit.

Chief Massasoit decided to come closer. He brought 20 men with him, but they left their bows and arrows behind. Captain Standish and another Pilgrim leader met the chief at the brook.

Chief Massasoit was much taller than Captain Standish, who certainly looked like Captain Shrimp next to the tall Native American. But Captain Standish showed no sign of being afraid. He stood at the chief's right side. He made sure he had several men behind him. He led the chief down the street. All the women and children of Plymouth watched. They were nervous and excited. Captain Standish focused on his job.

Captain Standish led Massasoit to a house that was almost finished. They put a green rug

Chief Massasoit met with the governor of Plymouth Colony, John Carver, and together they worked out a peace treaty.

and some cushions on the floor. Chief Massasoit sat down with the governor of Plymouth Colony. Together they decided to enter a peace **treaty**. They agreed they would not hurt each other. If anyone else tried to hurt either group, they would help each other. If the Native Americans stole any of the Pilgrims' tools, Massasoit would return the tools. Whenever the two groups met, they would leave their weapons behind.

This peace treaty lasted for 50 years. Because of it, Plymouth Colony could feel safe with their nearest Native American neighbors.

The next day, Massaoit invited the Pilgrim leaders to visit his camp. Captain Standish went with one other man, Isaac Allerton. They gave the Native Americans a kettle filled with English peas. Miles was satisfied that the Wampanoags would be friends to the Plymouth colony.

Squanto decided he wanted to stay with the settlers and help them. As a child he had lived in the same place the Pilgrims had settled. He had been in England when the rest of his tribe got sick and died. He had no people of his own. He was glad to stay at Plymouth.

Squanto acted as a translator whenever the people at Plymouth needed to talk to Massasoit.

He showed them the good places to fish, and taught them how to hunt deer and turkeys. He explained which plants were good to eat. The most important thing he did was show the settlers how to plant the corn they had found on their first discovery. The settlers planted their gardens as well as 26 acres of crops.

Because of Squanto's help, the Plymouth Colony had a very good harvest the next fall. They celebrated with a feast that they shared with the Indians. This was the first Thanksgiving. They thanked God for bringing them through their first year in the New World. Captain Standish and his small army marched and showed off their muskets. The whole colony celebrated the progress of the army.

Another Native American also joined the Pilgrims. Hobomok was one of Massasoit's men. He became a good friend to Miles Standish. Squanto was a close friend to William Bradford, one of the other leaders. Hobomok stayed in Plymouth and lived in Miles's house for many years.

When the settlers first arrived, they did not know what to expect from the Native Americans, nor did the Native Americans know what to expect from them. But gradually—especially with the help of Squanto and Hobomok—the Pilgrims and some of the Indians became friendly and learned to trust each other.

Ready for Everything

Squanto and Hobomok were a great help to the colony. And Chief Massasoit trusted the Pilgrims to keep their part of the treaty. But being friendly with a few Native Americans did not solve all the problems. Miles Standish and the other leaders were always thinking about how they could better protect themselves.

The new colony needed to be cautious of Native Americans who might not be as friendly as the Wampanoags. They also needed to protect their precious supplies. For the whole first year in the New World, they had no new supplies from England. They had to be very careful with everything they used.

Because he was the military captain, Miles Standish worked hard to protect the colony. He also traveled around the area trying to find supplies the colony could use. He traded with Native Americans and with other European groups for things like corn and fur. The colony also needed to gather goods that they could send back to England. They still owed money to the people who had sponsored them on the *Mayflower.*

Miles Standish's reputation for getting angry very quickly sometimes made people pay attention to him. But at other times it caused trouble with the groups he traded with. On one trading trip, Miles discovered that some beads and scissors had been stolen. He marched his army up to the door of the Native American leader. Angrily and firmly, he demanded that the items be returned by morning. The people in the tribe tried to entertain him and make him forget about the missing items. But Miles refused the entertainment. He camped for the night and waited. In the morning, the beads and scissors were returned, and the chief promised that the thief had been punished.

One summer day, Hobomok came running into Plymouth with news that Squanto might be dead. Hobomok and Squanto were visiting a chief named Corbitant, who did not like the English people. He was angry at Hobomok and Squanto because they were friends with the English. When Hobomok saw Corbitant try to stab Squanto, he ran for his life.

Captain Standish would not allow his friends to be threatened. He took 14 men and marched off to the place where Corbitant was. This was almost all of the men in Plymouth.

Hobomok showed the way. At night they crept into the sleeping village. They found the chief's hut and surrounded it. Then they burst into the hut, shouting, "Is Corbitant here?" But Corbitant was not there. The men from Plymouth found only frightened members of his family. Standish promised not to hurt anyone and said they only wanted Corbitant.

Meanwhile, Hobomok climbed to the roof of the hut. He shouted Squanto's name. In a few minutes, Squanto appeared, along with some other Native Americans. They were all frightened of Standish. Corbitant had run away, they explained. The men Corbitant left behind offered gifts to the Pilgrims as a way of saying they wanted peace.

No one was hurt that night. But what happened turned out to be very important. Many of the Native American tribes in the area heard about what happened. They did not want to battle against Standish and his small, fierce army. Nine Native American leaders came to Plymouth to seek peace.

But trouble between the Indians and Pilgrims continued. Massasoit told Hobomok about a plot against Plymouth and Wessagusset, another European settlement. Hobomok told Edward Winslow, one of the Pilgrims. According to the story, another Indian tribe was planning to attack Wessagusset and then Plymouth and kill everyone.

As soon as the news reached Plymouth, Standish organized a small group of men. He went to meet the plotting tribe and pretended that he wanted to trade with them. Standish became convinced the story was true. The men he met with were rude and insulting. They made threats against the English. Captain Standish believed that if he did not kill these Native Americans, they would kill everyone in Plymouth. Miles decided that he had to protect the Pilgrims by killing Wituwamat and the men who were with him. At the end of the night, seven Native Americans were dead.

Later it seemed that the story Hobomok had brought to Plymouth was not true. But it was too late.

This kind of tension with the Native Americans made Captain Standish very careful. The men of Plymouth had mounted their cannons on a wooden platform soon after they landed at Plymouth. Miles wanted a real fort. He directed the men to drag heavy oak timbers up the hill.

They built a square building with a flat roof. The cannons were mounted on the flat roof.

Miles also believed that Plymouth needed a **palisade** around the entire town. The people of Plymouth worked long and hard at the job. They built a fence that was 11 feet high and almost a mile long, going all the way around the small town. It protected their new homes, as well as the brook from which they got their water.

Miles organized the Pilgrim army into four groups. Each group had its own commander, and each group guarded one of the four walls of the palisade in times of danger. Captain Standish drilled the men and made them practice. He wanted to be sure they would know exactly what to do if they were attacked.

One group was also assigned special duty in case of fire. Miles instructed them to circle the burning building with their backs to the fire and their muskets ready. Not every fire was an accident.

The *Mayflower* was not the only ship to bring

Despite friendships between the settlers and certain tribes, there were often hostilities between the colonists and the Native Americans. Miles Standish organized the Pilgrim army so they would be prepared in case of attack.

settlers to the New World. The first winter was long and lonely for the Pilgrims, but then more ships began to arrive. Miles had to be prepared for the danger that new ships might bring. The first time a new ship arrived, he put his plan into action. When he received a message that a ship with a tall white sail was approaching, he got ready. The cannon on Fort Hill boomed a warning. Standish got his army ready.

Of course the growing colony needed more people, especially after so many died during the first winter. But they needed supplies even more. When the *Fortune* arrived, it brought people but no supplies—no food, no clothing, no ammunition, no seed, no work animals. Now the Pilgrims had to share what little they had with even more people.

The ship turned out to be the *Fortune,* and it carried people who wanted to join the colony. Some of the passengers were Separatists who had been in Holland. Now they were reunited with friends and family in Plymouth.

In 1623, three years after the *Mayflower,* the *Anne* arrived. This ship was important to Miles Standish, because it carried Barbara, who soon became his new wife. Barbara might have been the sister of Miles's first wife, Rose, so perhaps he had known her in England. They married and soon had five children: Alexander, Myles, Josiah, Charles, and Lora.

Miles had come to Plymouth as a Stranger who was hired to lead their army. Now he had truly made Plymouth his home.

Although Miles remained a Stranger and never joined the Pilgrims' church, he was a highly respected member of the community and church services were even held in his fort.

A Life of Service

The Separatists who came on the *Mayflower* wanted the new town to be a religious place. Plymouth Colony had a rule that said all the citizens of the colony must be members of the Pilgrims' church. Only members of the church could be leaders or make decisions about Plymouth.

Miles Standish never joined the Pilgrims' church. Yet he was allowed to be both a citizen and a leader. He was the only one who did not have to follow this rule. Perhaps the Pilgrims knew how much they needed his leadership. Perhaps they appreciated how well he worked to protect them. Captain Miles Standish was important to the beginning of Plymouth. He continued to be important for many years. Being a Stranger instead of a Saint never held him back.

Even though he never joined the church, Miles did worship with the Pilgrims. In fact, worship services were held in his fort. The Pilgrims had a formal ceremony for marching to the church services. They marched three across, led by a sergeant. Each man wore a cloak and carried a musket. Behind them walked Governor William Bradford, wearing a long robe. On his right side was the preacher. On his left side was Miles Standish. Once inside the fort, the men kept their guns nearby.

Miles was the commander of the army at Plymouth for more than 30 years. The army was never very big. But Miles acted as if it was the biggest army of the greatest country. He trained the men well. He was very serious about this job.

Miles had many other jobs as well. In 1624 he became one of the assistant governors, a job he held for most of his life. He was also the treasurer

For safety, the Pilgrims marched to church in a
carefully planned formation, walking three
across and carrying their muskets.

With his fierce temper and military training, Miles was the natural choice to lead the Pilgrims' army, but he also served the colony in many other ways.

of Plymouth near the end of his life. For five years the fiery captain collected taxes, paid bills, and kept accounts.

A few years after Plymouth was settled,

Miles became a representative for the colony. The governor sent him to England in 1625. The adventurers who had given the settlers money and supplies in 1620 were unhappy. They did not think that the settlers were paying back the debt fast enough. Miles was sent to London to meet with the adventurers. Everyone knew Miles had a bad temper. The governor warned him not to cause trouble. It was Miles's job to convince the people in England that the settlers needed more supplies, and that they had to be cheaper.

Standish spent several months in London. The city was full of sickness, and anyone who could afford to go to the countryside did. There were not very many people with whom Miles could do business. But he managed to learn some news to take back to Plymouth. King James I was dead. Even more important to the Pilgrims was news about their pastor John Robinson, who had sent them from Holland to the New World. The Pilgrims had expected that he would soon be coming to join them. Miles had to tell them the sad news that Pastor Robinson was dead. Although they had been separated for several years, the Saints at Plymouth grieved for John Robinson.

Soon after the trip to London, Miles Standish became even more important to Plymouth. He had not reached his goal in London. He did not get better prices for supplies. But this was the beginning of an idea to solve the Pilgrims' problems another way.

Standish and a few other men became **undertakers** for Plymouth. This meant that they would be responsible for the debt of the colony. The Pilgrims in Plymouth and the adventurers in England agreed on an amount that would settle the debt. Then the Pilgrims would not owe any more money to England. After that, they could keep all the money they earned in Plymouth.

The undertakers promised that they would pay the debt. The rest of the people in Plymouth

The population of Plymouth was quite small at first but gradually the town grew and the settlers began to spread out, increasing their building and their planting. Here a gardener at Plimouth Plantation works the land.

To commemorate the 300th anniversary of the Pilgrims' arrival, a plaque in Provincetown, Massachusetts, marks the shore where the Pilgrims first landed, led by (among others) Miles Standish.

would not have to pay the debt. The undertakers were in charge of deciding what to do with the furs, corn, beads, knives, and other goods that the Pilgrims had. They could establish new trading posts and use Plymouth's boats to reach them. They built trading posts to the north, the south, and the west of Plymouth. The people of Plymouth agreed to this plan. They signed a contract to let the undertakers take care of Plymouth's business. It took six years of hard work for the undertakers to pay off the debt.

At first Plymouth's population did not grow very quickly. They had fewer than 200 people when the undertakers took over the debt. But gradually the town grew. As Plymouth became more settled, the settlers began to spread out. Miles helped to begin a new town, called Duxbury, which was across the harbor from Plymouth. For many years the people attended church in Plymouth, but eventually they decided to organize their own church.

The Standish family was one of the families that moved to Duxbury. Miles Standish's sons went on to become leaders in the town. Two of them married daughters of Pilgrim families, even though their parents never joined the church. One of his sons became a leader in the Duxbury church.

On October 3, 1656, Captain Miles Standish died. He was 70 years old and had become very sick. In his will he asked to be buried in Duxbury. He wanted to be buried near his daughter, Lora, who had died earlier.

It was easy to make Captain Shrimp mad. He often let himself get too angry. He did not always care about getting along with other people. But he did care very much about Plymouth. On the *Mayflower,* he was a Stranger. The Pilgrims always officially considered him a Stranger. But his heart belonged to Plymouth colony.

GLOSSARY

adventurer a person who helps to sponsor a new colony or business

colony a settlement in a new land by a group of people who leave their country

Church of England the established part of the Christian Church in England; the Puritans did not agree with everything in the Church of England

flintlock a piece of flint in part of the musket to strike a spark and fire the musket

lean-to a small addition to one side of a house

Mayflower Compact an agreement signed by the Pilgrims about how they would be governed

musket the kind of shoulder-carried guns soldiers used before rifles were invented

palisade a long wooden fence made of tall wooden stakes

Pilgrim a person who journeys to a foreign land for religious reasons

Puritan a person who practices a strict religious belief

Saint a religious Separatist who made the journey on the *Mayflower*

Separatists a group of Puritans who broke off from the main group

GLOSSARY

shallop a small, lightweight boat that could be rowed or sailed

Stranger a term used by the Puritans to described the people who traveled on the *Mayflower* who were not religious

treaty an agreement between two groups of people not to fight

undertaker one of the people who took on the debt of the Plymouth Colony so they would not owe money to the adventurers

wattle and daub rods and twigs covered with earth and clay, used to build a house

CHRONOLOGY

1584	Miles Standish is born in Chorley, Lancashire, England.
1608	The Pilgrims move from England to Leiden, in the Netherlands, under the leadership of John Robinson.
1617	The Pilgrims decide to leave the Netherlands for North America.
1620	The Pilgrims land at Provincetown in November and discover Plymouth Harbor in December.
1621	On January 14 the common house burns. Rose Standish dies on January 29. In April the Pilgrims and the Indians make a peace treaty. Together they celebrate the first Thanksgiving that autumn.
1623	Miles marries Barbara; they eventually have five children.
1625–26	Miles goes to England and learns of John Robinson's death.
1627	Miles and several other leaders take on the colony's debt so it can be independent.
1631	Miles helps to found the town of Duxbury, Massachusetts.

CHRONOLOGY

1624–47   Miles Standish serves as a governor's assistant in Plymouth Colony.

1652–55   Miles serves as treasurer of the Plymouth colony.

1656   Miles Standish dies on October 3.

COLONIAL TIME LINE

1607 Jamestown, Virginia, is settled by the English.

1620 Pilgrims on the *Mayflower* land at Plymouth, Massachusetts.

1623 The Dutch settle New Netherland, the colony that later becomes New York.

1630 Massachusetts Bay Colony is started.

1634 Maryland is settled as a Roman Catholic colony. Later Maryland becomes a safe place for people with different religious beliefs.

1636 Roger Williams is thrown out of the Massachusetts Bay Colony. He settles Rhode Island, the first colony to give people freedom of religion.

1682 William Penn forms the colony of Pennsylvania.

1688 Pennsylvania Quakers make the first formal protest against slavery.

1692 Trials for witchcraft are held in Salem, Massachusetts.

COLONIAL TIME LINE

1712 Slaves revolt in New York. Twenty-one blacks are killed as punishment.

1720 Major smallpox outbreak occurs in Boston. Cotton Mather and some doctors try a new treatment. Many people think the new treatment shouldn't be used.

1754 French and Indian War begins. It ends nine years later.

1761 Benjamin Banneker builds a wooden clock that keeps precise time.

1765 Britain passes the Stamp Act. Violent protests break out in the colonies. The Stamp Act is ended the next year.

1775 The battles of Lexington and Concord begin the American Revolution.

1776 Declaration of Independence is signed.

FURTHER READING

Dunnaboo, Terry. *Plimouth Plantation*. City: Dillon Press, 1995.

George, Jean Craighead. *The First Thanksgiving*. New York: Pilomel, 1993.

McGovern, Ann. *If You Sailed on the Mayflower in 1620*. New York: Scholastic, 1991.

Reece, Colleen L. *Plymouth Pioneers*. Uhrichsville, Ohio: Barbour Publishing, 1997.

Roop, Connie, and Peter Roop, eds. *Pilgrim Voices: Our First Year in the New World*. New York: Walker and Company, 1995.

Sewall, Marcia. *The Pilgrims of Plimoth*. New York: Atheneum Press, 1986.

Stein, R. Conrad. *The Pilgrims*. Chicago: Childrens Press, 1995.

INDEX

INDEX

and Mayflower Compact, 18
as military leader, 31, 32–33, 35,
    47–52, 54, 55, 58
and Native Americans, 24–25,
    31–33, 35, 40–44, 45, 47–51
parents of, 7
and Pilgrim's church, 57–58
as representative to England,
    60–62
as soldier in England, 8–9, 10, 20
temper of, 12, 48–49, 61, 66
and Thanksgiving, 45
as treasurer, 58, 60
and voyage to Provincetown,
    10–11, 12, 15

wives of. *See* Standish, Rose; Stan-
    dish, Barbara
Standish, Rose (first wife), 10, 33,
    34, 55
Strangers, 11–12, 17

Thanksgiving, 45

Wampanoag tribe, 39–40, 42, 44,
    47. *See also* Native Americans
Wessagusset, 50
Winslow, Edward, 50
Wituwamat, 51

PICTURE CREDITS

ABOUT THE AUTHORS

SUSAN MARTINS MILLER started reading historical stories when she was nine years old. She has written more than 25 books for children and adults. Her books include fiction, nonfiction, and biography. She lives in Colorado Springs, Colorado, with her husband and two children.

Senior Consulting Editor **ARTHUR M. SCHLESINGER, JR.** is the leading American historian of our time. He won the Pulitzer Prize for his book *The Age of Jackson* (1945) and again for *A Thousand Days* (1965). This chronicle of the Kennedy Administration also won a National Book Award. He has written many other books including a multi-volume series, *The Age of Roosevelt*. Professor Schlesinger is the Albert Schweitzer Professor of the Humanities at the City University of New York, and has been involved in several other Chelsea House projects, including the REVOLUTIONARY WAR LEADERS biographies on the most prominent figures of early American history.

2/01

GAYLORD S

ML